MarketingFundamentals

Roadmap for how to develop, implement, and measure a successful marketing plan.

By: Mark Nelson

Disclaimer

This ebook has been written for information purposes only. Every effort has been made to make this ebook as complete and accurate as possible. However, there may be mistakes in typography or content. Also, this ebook provides information only up to the publishing date. Therefore, this ebook should be used as a guide - not as the ultimate source.

The purpose of this ebook is to educate. The author and the publisher do not warrant that the information contained in this ebook is fully complete and shall not be responsible for any errors or omissions. The author and publisher shall have neither liability nor responsibility to any person or entity with respect to any loss or damage caused or alleged to be caused directly or indirectly by this ebook.

Table of Contents

Disclaimer 3

Introduction 5

1: Understanding Marketing's Role 6

2: Analyzing your Business 11

3: Developing Your Strategy 20

4: Developing the Tactical Phase 25

5: Aligning the Organization 36

6. Launching and Measuring your Plan 39

7.Conclusion 44

Introduction

Whether you're marketing a new product, a new service, or even marketing yourself, you'll be more successful if you follow a structured process. After all, there's a lot at stake when you're trying to market something, In this course, I'll share with you a framework for analyzing a market, developing effective strategies, and creating tactical marketing programs that link to your strategy.

I'll also share how to run the marketing planning process and how to organize a cross-functional team to help you create a marketing plan. If you work in the marketing function now, this course can help you sharpen your skills and add more depth to your current programs. If you're thinking about moving into marketing as a career, understanding the marketing planning process is an essential first step. Marketing is an exciting field, but it has to be practiced responsibly and ethically.

Through the concepts I'll share with you in this course, you'll begin to develop the skills that'll help you do just that.

1: Understanding Marketing's Role

Marketing in an organization

So what is marketing? The American Marketing Association, or AMA, defines it as the activity, set of institutions, and processes for creating, communicating, delivering, and exchanging offerings. That have value for customers, clients, partners, and society at large. Well, that's quite a mouthful. For me, marketing is simply this. It's all about changing beliefs in the minds of customers.

Every organization has customers, regardless of whether you're a commercial for-profit firm, or a non-profit. All companies must be seen as relevant to those customers if they want to survive. Marketing then, is getting customers to believe that your products and services are important, and that they deliver a better value than the competition's. Smart companies see marketing as an investment. That's because the marketing function may be the most critical in any organization.

Marketing is how companies wage competitive battle in the marketplace. If a company doesn't fight the good fight, it won't be around long. Companies that excel at marketing not only survive, but they grow in value. But marketing is hard work. It's a world of ambiguity, and constant challenge. Think about the things that change for a company. For example, consumer trends. New generations of consumers, millennials for example, have different needs than previous generations.

A good marketer has to adapt to that. Competition changes, new competitors enter the market, and the old competitors try new things to take your customers away. Marketers are also affected by changes in technology. Innovations in new products, as well as new ways to connect to customers, especially social media, have a dramatic impact on the marketing function. But companies are also affected by external factors, like political climate, economic conditions, as well as the regulatory environment.

A sudden downturn in the economy, stiffer regulations in your industry, or a surprise election result, might impact consumer behavior. You can't predict these changes, but you can adapt to them if you have two things. A well thought out marketing strategy, and a written marketing plan. A marketing strategy defines which customers you're going after. And how you'll change their beliefs about your products and services. Your marketing plan outlines the specific steps you'll take to implement your strategy.

Having both helps you prepare for the unexpected, so you can adapt and refine your marketing programs as needed. Within an organization, think of the marketing function as the hub of a wheel. Connected to that hub are all the other activities within that company. Operations, sales, finance, and so on. The marketing function coordinates all these other activities to create value for customers. It takes talented, well trained people, led by experienced marketing leaders.

Look at the most successful companies today, and you'll find that they invest in training to keep their marketing skills strong, and that's what this course is all about.

Understanding the planning process

President Dwight Eisenhower once said, plans are nothing, planning is everything. There's a lot of truth to that. Although you'll come out of this process with a written document, it's the planning process itself that allows you to learn about your competitive situation, to make tough choices, and to align your team. You can start the process any time, but an important consideration is how and when your company does its annual business planning process.

That's where the company develops financial forecasts, investments, budgets and so on. Now, generally speaking, there are two ways to connect the marketing planning with the business planning. Some companies start the marketing planning process first. Right around the middle of the fiscal year. Each marketing team develops their own sales revenue forecast, for their assigned products. They also develop a budget to spend on marketing programs that they think are needed to achieve those revenue forecasts.

Those forecasts and budgets are combined into a company-level revenue forecast and budget. And that's fed directly into the annual business planning process. Now some companies do just the opposite. They start with the business planning process, where they develop an overall revenue goal and spending target, and then those are divided and given to the individual marketing teams. Those teams now have to take those targets and develop the best marketing plan they can to achieve those goals.

The marketing planning process has four phases. In the analysis phase, you'll learn about your customers in terms of how and why they buy your product. You'll analyze the competition, and how they compare to your company in terms of strengths and weaknesses. You'll also analyze the overall market, to understand its potential. And where the most attractive segments of the market are, to earn revenue. In the strategy phase, you'll use what you've learned to make decisions around segmenting the market, targeting specific parts of those segments.

And ultimately, how you will position your products and services to win over customers. In the tactical phase, you'll create marketing programs to execute your strategy. You'll make decisions around your products and services, and how they have to perform in delivering benefits to your customers. You'll set prices. You'll create sales support material. And you'll develop a marketing communications campaign. And finally is the measurement phase. As the name implies, this is the part of the process where you find out if you're achieving what you expected to achieve.

But it's not just measuring sales. It's finding out if you're getting business from the customers you expected to get business from, and it's also finding out if they bought your products and services for the reasons you expected. The measurement phase helps you know if you're getting a good return on your marketing investments. A good marketer is disciplined, and doesn't cut corners in the planning process. It takes time and lots of hard work, but in the end, it's worth it.

Assembling the team

Good marketers know the value of a diverse and talented team of colleagues to help develop and execute their marketing strategy. You'll need to draw on their expertise, their market knowledge, possibly their resources, and their network. Your team will include colleagues inside the company, as well as external partners, like advertising and promotional firms. Let's review the various roles of your cross functional team. First is finance.

Your finance department plays a very important role in making sure you have sufficient budget dollars to execute your plan. Now it may at times feel like the finance guys are there just to cut your budget, but believe me, they want you to succeed. After all, the marketing effort is the key to achieving revenue goals. Without your efforts, budgets might have to shrink even smaller, making their job even tougher. Finance partners will also help you in the measurement phase of the planning process. They'll help you quantify your ROMI, return on marketing investments.

And they'll help find ways to improve it, in the next business cycle. Marketing research is another key role you'll need in your team. Your company may have a separate marketing research department, or it may outsource it. But either way, you'll need their help understanding customer needs, testing new product concepts, or perhaps testing a new advertising message. Marketing research can be applied at just about every step of the marketing process. So, be sure to get their advice on the best way to use this important resource.

Next is your technical team. These are the people who develop your products and services. They might be engineers or scientists in an R&D department. Or perhaps software developers. It depends on the nature of your business. You'll need their help making sure your products and services deliver the right benefits to delight your customers. Speaking of delighting customers, be sure to involve your design team. In many companies, design is a separate department. And they can help make sure your products and services are delivering the right experience for your customers, to build and enhance the brand promise.

Most companies have a sales function, and you should enlist their help in developing a marketing plan. After all, they're on the front line, day to day. And they have a lot of insight about your customers, and your competition. They'll have ideas about the selling tools they need to succeed. Be sure to get their input. Depending on your business, you may also want to involve colleagues from manufacturing or operations. These are the people who make the products and deliver the service.

A customer support team for example, might have great insights about customer complaints or service issues. External partners might include your advertising agency.

Your branding company, a public relations firm. And perhaps a marketing consultant. They're there to help you succeed. So, make them a part of the team from the very start. Once you've identified the key players on your team, make sure they're aware of your planning schedule. That they know their role, and they know the expectations that you have for each other in developing a great marketing strategy.

Creating the marketing plan

- A formal written marketing plan is a great way to document the planning process. It serves many purposes. First, it captures all the things you and your team have learned about the market, the competition, and your customers. This information is critical, because it becomes the supporting evidence for the strategies that you and your team decide to pursue. Second, the plan serves as a tool to help you align the organization. Marketing involves many people, so you'll need to get everyone on board and going in the same direction.

The written plan becomes a source document to create presentations, to conduct training, and to give directions to external partners. Believe me, you'll use it a lot. Finally, the written plan lays out a coherent and coordinated set of marketing programs with schedules and budgets, so you can run a smooth operation. Now, there are many formats you can use for the written plan, but most plans will include the following components.

An executive summary that gives a brief, high level review of the plan. The situation analysis that documents all the data about your company's strengths and weaknesses, the market opportunity, the competition, and of course, the customer. The strategy section that outlines how you segment the market, who you plan to target and how you will position your products and services in the market. The tactical programs, including what products you will offer, what prices you will charge, how you will promote your products, and how you'll distribute them.

A financial section that documents your revenue projections and budget requirements. An implementation plan that outlines the timing of your programs and who's responsible. Now, to write the plan, don't wait until the very end of the planning process. I like to start writing it from the very beginning. Here's a tip that makes that easy. Create a blank PowerPoint presentation with just the headings of each component on a separate page.

Keep it with you during team meetings. As you collect information or make key decisions, write or type that into the appropriate slide. That helps you keep the document up-to-date as you move through the process. When you have enough written material, go ahead and create a first draft, but be sure to date the draft, as you'll be making regular updates and revisions. A written marketing plan is a dynamic document, and you should expect to make changes to it as conditions in the market change.

If you create a great plan and update it regularly, it'll help you stay ahead of the competition.

Understanding B2B vs. B2C marketing

In marketing, you'll often hear the terms B2B and B2C. B2B means business to business. That's where your business is selling products and services to other businesses. B2C stands for business to consumer, where you're selling goods and services to everyday people, like you and me. As you begin the marketing planning process, it's important to know the key differences between the two. Keep in mind that the marketing planning process is exactly the same for each.

But how you execute certain steps in the process will vary. Let's explore how. When people buy products and services, they're buying a collection of benefits. And you can categorize those benefits into three types. Functional benefits refer to a product's physical performance. For example, when buying a car, functional benefits include the size of the engine. Passenger seating, or how the car handles. Economic benefits are related to saving money or saving time.

With the car, economic benefits would include the miles per gallon, the annual maintenance costs, or the car's reliability. And finally our emotional benefits. These are related to the psychological feelings you get, when using a product. For a car, it would include things like status, or self-esteem. Perhaps the biggest difference between B2B and B2C marketing is what types of benefits are most important.

For consumers, emotional benefits tend to be most important, while for companies, the economic cost savings and other financial factors will drive their decisions. Let's go back to our car example. When consumers like you and me buy a car, we look for something that matches our personality and taste. We want to feel good in that new car. Once we've satisfied that need, then we make sure we get the functional and economic benefits. But for a company, buying a car for an employee, the situation is completely opposite.

The other key difference is who's involved in the purchasing process. In B2B marketing, companies usually have a purchasing department buy goods and services. The person involved won't be the one who actually consumes the product or service. So they're more logical and unemotional when they make buying decisions. That will affect how you market to them. Consumers, on the other hand, usually buy products for themselves, or for others. They make the buying decisions themselves. Now, they, too, can be quite logical for some purchases, but there's usually an emotional involvement here too.

You'll need to understand these emotions to develop effective marketing strategies. I'll show you how to do that when we discuss the analysis phase, of the planning process, coming up next.

2: Analyzing your Business

Focusing on your core business

It may sound obvious, but the first step to developing a marketing plan is to know what business you're in. How you decide that can have a big impact on the size of the market you compete in, and the intensity of competition you face. You can define your core business very broadly, or very narrowly. Let's imagine you're a manufacturer of high quality men's wallets. And you sell a variety of thin leather wallets in many countries worldwide.

Now, you could define your core business narrowly, just thin leather wallets, for example. Or you could broaden the scope just a bit, and say your core business is wallets in general. In that case, you would make wallets of any size, shape, and material. If you kicked it up another notch, your core business could be defined as products that carry things. Defining this way would change your perspective a lot. Now you might expand into things like purses, backpacks, luggage, and so on.

Or, you could define your entire core business around a primary benefit. For example, we're in the core business of making things that are slim. In this very broad case, that would completely change your strategic perspective. You would consider offering a wide variety of products that all have this unique benefit of slim. Slim wallets, slim purses, slim clothes, slim anything. Notice that with each change in the core business definition, the size of the business opportunity gets bigger.

That might sound like the way to go. The bigger the better right? Not necessarily. With each increasing level of opportunity comes more challenge. You have more competition to consider. But perhaps even more important, is that you have to be good at so many other things. You have to decide whether it's better to focus on the things that you do really well, and deliver that consistently to your customers. Or, you may want to expand as broadly as you can, and try to grow the business.

My advice is to define your core business just up to the point where you can still leverage your core skills, or what are called core competencies. If you try to do things that you're not skilled at doing, you'll run into trouble.

Determining your marketing plan's scope

You can write a marketing plan for one specific product or service, a collection of products or services, or for the company's entire family of products and services. You should decide this before you start the planning work. Because how you decide has a dramatic impact on how you go about marketing. When you develop a marketing plan for a single product, the entire focus is on all the resources and activities needed to get just that product into the hands of prospective customers.

All your decisions about how you communicate, sell, and set prices, are about that product only, even if you have other products to offer. That might make sense, especially for a brand new product. But, sometimes it makes more sense to develop your marketing strategy around a family of products, or even all of them. It's usually much more efficient to spread your marketing dollars across all of your products than concentrating on just one. So how do you decide? You don't.

The customer decides this for you. Why do I say that? Because in marketing, we always want to take the customer's perspective. You may be selling a product, but your identity in the customer's mind is represented by brands. Regardless of whether you're marketing to consumers or to businesses, your brand is how customers understand you. Therefore, we base our decision from the outside looking in. A brand is essentially the promise that you are making to the customer to deliver a set of benefits.

Brands usually have an identity, in the form of a distinctive logo, or a name. If your company and products are known by one brand, such as McDonald's, then it would make sense to develop your strategy at this level of the firm. If your company is not well known to customers, but they know your product's brand names very well, then it makes sense to develop your plan around each specific brand. For example, when consumers go to the grocery store, they generally don't ask, hey, can you tell me where the Proctor & Gamble toothpaste is? No, instead they look for the much more familiar brand name called Crest toothpaste.

In marketing, we call this the brand architecture. A branded house is the single brand under which all your products and services are marketed. Companies like Chase, BMW, are considered umbrella brands. At the other end of the spectrum is house of brands, such as P&P and Unilever, with many well known individual brands. In the middle are hybrids. The endorser brands, like Marriott, use the good Marriott name to endorse individual hotel brands like Courtyard and Fairfield Inn.

You've heard the old saying, the customer is always right. When deciding on what level to write your plan, take their advice, and write the plan around how they understand you, and your family of brands.

Researching the competition

Marketing would be relatively easy, if it were not for the fact that you always face some type of competition. A competitor is anything that wants the same thing that you do. It can be an individual, a company, or even a completely unrelated activity that distracts your potential customers away from you. You need to understand your competition for a lot of reasons. First, you need to know which ones to focus on, and which ones to avoid.

You want to stay away from a competitor if they are much stronger than you. If you take customers away from a stronger competitor, you may trigger a reaction from them that you aren't prepared to handle. The intensity of competition will affect the overall potential for success of your business. This is why it's important to consider all types of competition when planning your business, to ensure that you have the edge over others in your industry. You need to compare your strengths and weaknesses to theirs to see how you match up.

This will help you select the right strategy to win. Competitors come in three different types. Direct, indirect, and what are called substitutes. A direct competitor is anyone who is selling the same things you are, and delivering the same benefit. An indirect competitor sells similar products, with different benefits. A substitute is any unrelated product or service, that a consumer can use in place of your products or services.

Let's look at the wallet industry. A maker of slim wallets competes directly with any wallet maker that also emphasizes the slim features of its products. Indirect competitors are makers of other wallets or other money-storing products with different benefits. And substitutes would include a plain old pocket to keep your stuff in. A good way to analyze the competition is with a tool called a competitive matrix, like the one you see here.

To create a matrix, list your company and your competitors across the top. Down the side, list the things that you want to compare. Things like size, market share, strengths and weaknesses, and especially the key strategy elements, like the value propositions. What does each company have in terms of key resources, and how do they use those resources to acquire and retain customers? A competitive matrix will vary a lot depending on the industry.

If you're in a high tech industry, you'll want to compare R&D activities, like spending, number of engineers, or number of new products launched. In service industries, be sure to compare things like how each company delivers the service. How they train their employees. Or, how they're rated for their service. Every industry has certain key factors that every competitor has to pay attention to. So, it's likely those factors will be the ones you want to compare. A word of caution. When you collect competitive information, use only information that is publicly available.

Never try to get inside information about your competitor that they would consider confidential. When you complete the matrix, take a close look at it and find some insights that you'll need later when deciding on your strategy. What conclusions can you draw from the matrix? By considering all the possible ways your customer's needs can be satisfied, and creating a strategy for handling the competition, you'll create powerful advantages in the marketplace.

Analyzing your products

When consumers use a product or service, they do so because they seek the bundle of benefits that a particular product or service delivers. Take a look at this ordinary drill bit. When you go to the hardware store to buy the drill bit, what are you actually buying? The drill bit? No. It's the hole that the drill bit will make that you're actually buying. The hole is the benefit of the drill bit. But we can take this idea of benefits even further.

Why do you need the hole? So you can hang that picture of you winning that special award at work. Keep going. Why do you want to hang that picture of you? So you can stay motivated to keep doing a great job. You may not have realized it, but you bought that drill bit to advance your career. Sound crazy? In marketing we call this Feature Benefit Laddering. Take a look at this example. Think of the steps of a ladder. At the bottom rung is your product.

Right above that are its main features, sharp spiraling edges, length, material, and so on. Then, above each feature is the primary benefit it delivers. In the case of a drill bit, that is simply a hole. Keep going, and you see that you can do a lot of things with a hole, including hanging a picture, and so on. We do this so we can understand how our product delivers value to the customer. Later, we'll use it to test whether consumers understand our product.

That might affect how we communicate to them. Let's create a feature benefit letter for a maker of high quality men's wallets. You start by listing all the product's features along the bottom. Then for each feature you write the benefit it delivers for each benefit you list the value it delivers. By value I mean the motivation a consumer would have for wanting the product. Our completed ladder looks like this. It's a bit like unpacking your product or service so you can see what the various features actually deliver.

To complete the product analysis, you need to test each feature of your product compared to the same feature on your competitor's products. You need to determine which feature performed better than the competition, which performed the same, and which performed not as well. When you complete the analysis, take a close look. Are there features that need to be improved? Are there certain competitors you want to avoid or possibly go after based on product performance? Later on, you'll be choosing a high-performing feature and its benefits to base your marketing strategy on.

Here's why. When you outperform the competition on a feature that is important to consumers and they know it, guess what? You earn a lot of customers. And that's what good marketing is all about.

Analyzing your products

When consumers use a product or service, they do so because they seek the bundle of benefits that a particular product or service delivers. Take a look at this ordinary drill bit. When you go to the hardware store to buy the drill bit, what are you actually buying? The drill bit? No. It's the hole that the drill bit will make that you're actually buying. The hole is the benefit of the drill bit. But we can take this idea of benefits even further.

Why do you need the hole? So you can hang that picture of you winning that special award at work. Keep going. Why do you want to hang that picture of you? So you can stay motivated to keep doing a great job. You may not have realized it, but you bought that drill bit to advance your career. Sound crazy? In marketing we call this Feature

Benefit Laddering. Take a look at this example. Think of the steps of a ladder. At the bottom rung is your product.

Right above that are its main features, sharp spiraling edges, length, material, and so on. Then, above each feature is the primary benefit it delivers. In the case of a drill bit, that is simply a hole. Keep going, and you see that you can do a lot of things with a hole, including hanging a picture, and so on. We do this so we can understand how our product delivers value to the customer. Later, we'll use it to test whether consumers understand our product.

That might affect how we communicate to them. Let's create a feature benefit letter for a maker of high quality men's wallets. You start by listing all the product's features along the bottom. Then for each feature you write the benefit it delivers for each benefit you list the value it delivers. By value I mean the motivation a consumer would have for wanting the product. Our completed ladder looks like this. It's a bit like unpacking your product or service so you can see what the various features actually deliver.

To complete the product analysis, you need to test each feature of your product compared to the same feature on your competitor's products. You need to determine which feature performed better than the competition, which performed the same, and which performed not as well. When you complete the analysis, take a close look. Are there features that need to be improved? Are there certain competitors you want to avoid or possibly go after based on product performance? Later on, you'll be choosing a high-performing feature and its benefits to base your marketing strategy on.

Here's why. When you outperform the competition on a feature that is important to consumers and they know it, guess what? You earn a lot of customers. And that's what good marketing is all about.

Analyzing your customers

Marketing is about acquiring and retaining customers. So, you absolutely have to have a thorough understanding of who they are, where they are, what they believe about your products and services, and how they go about purchasing them. Good customer analysis starts with deciding on exactly what is as customer. How you define a customer will have a big impact on how you go about reaching them. You can define them very broadly or you can make the definition very narrow and specific.

For example, let's look at the market for wallets. A broad definition of a customer would be anyone who has a need to carry money or credit cards. In that case, just about anyone is a potential customer. You could be more specific and define it around purchase behavior. A customer is anyone who's going to replace their wallet within a year. You can even be more specific and define a customer around their attitudes and brand loyalty.

In that case, you might say a customer is anyone who uses a specific brand of wallet and would recommend it to others. With this definition, we have fewer total customers, but now we have a very focused and identifiable group of people to market to. Once you define a customer, you need to understand what's going on in their minds in terms of what's important to them and what perceptions they have about your products and services versus the competition. Customers buy things for a variety of reasons.

But some are more important than others. If you know what's most important to them, you can appeal to that need when trying to get them to buy, or you can try to raise the sense of importance they place on another factor. You also need to measure how they rate your product versus others and how it delivers each benefit. They may have misperceptions that you need to change. You may be able to emphasize a key feature of your product that is better than the competition. This analysis would be critical later when you begin segmenting customers.

For our wallet example, let's imagine we did some marketing research and created this customer analysis. We ask customers to rate the importance of each buying factor on a scale of one to ten, where ten is the highest. We also ask them to rate their perception of each brand of wallet and how it delivers on that buying factor on a scale of one to ten. Let's find out what we can learn from this analysis. First, the buying factor of slimness is rated the highest and that's good news for a manufacturer of wallets that are slim.

Because they're perceived by customers as being the best at making slim wallets. But notice, this hypothetical company is not rated the highest in every buying factor. For example, with capacity, the competition's wallet is perceived as holding more stuff, and having more color choices. Prices also rated higher for the competition. Meaning, they're perceived to have a lower priced wallet. What this means for our hypothetical company is, they need to stick to their primary claim of slim.

And avoid making comparisons to the competitors where they're not as well rated. In many ways, great marketers understand their customers better than they understand themselves. A solid customer analysis prepares you to develop solid marketing strategy.

Analyzing the buying process

- Customers follow a distinct set of steps when buying anything. That process may take a matter of seconds, such as an impulse purchase at a store, or it may take a matter of months, such as the purchase of a new home or a car. Typically though these steps are as follows: First is the Need Recognition phase. This is where customers realize that they want something. That can be triggered internally, for example if a customer is thirsty that will trigger a need for some type of beverage.

But it can also be triggered externally through advertising or other stimuli. If a customer sees a TV commercial for a cold soft drink or perhaps sees a group of people drinking it, those could stimulate the customer to want that same drink. The Need Recognition step is very important because without it there won't be a sale. The next step is Information Search. Once customers feel a need to have something, they start gathering information about solutions for that need.

They get information from a wide variety of sources including commercial advertising, Internet search, while shopping in a store, and most importantly from other customers. This is a critical step because this is where a customer is most receptive to your marketing message. Once a customer gathers information they go to the next step, which is to evaluate the alternatives. Customers make choices based on two things, what features are most important and which brand does the best job in delivering those benefits? Customers will make head-to-head comparisons between your product and the competition, so it's critical that you give them a complete picture of how your product will best satisfy their needs.

Eventually the customer will narrow their choices down to one brand, and they'll go to the next step, the Purchase phase. Buying a product may take a matter of seconds, such as buying a soft drink at a vending machine, or it could take months that might involve negotiations, financing, training, maybe installation. Complex, expensive products usually take a lot longer to buy than your everyday consumer good that you'd find in a grocery store. Now you might think that the buying process ends here with the final purchase, but there's one last step.

It's called the Post-Purchase Behavior phase. Once customers start using the product or service, they compare the results with their expectations. Did the product work as expected? How did the product make them feel when they used it? This phase is also critical because customers will share their experiences, good or bad, with other customers. And with the way information spreads through social media that can be really helpful or hurtful to your marketing campaign.

Something else happens at this phase that a marketer needs to be aware of. It's called Buyer's Remorse. Customers might start having second thoughts on whether it was a good idea to buy the product. They start to wonder, "Gee, did I pay too much? "Did I really need this product? "Was there a better alternative out there "that I should have bought instead?" Marketers need to weigh in at this phase and remind the customer that they made a great choice. You can do that with advertising.

For example, many of the car commercials you see on TV are directed at the people who already bought that specific model. These commercials let the customer see what they look like to others when driving the car so they feel they made a smart decision to buy that model. But you don't need expensive TV commercials to do this. Post-Purchase follow up could be as simple as a phone call or perhaps an email to your customer. Either way you don't want to just assume your customer is satisfied.

Reach out and find out. Great marketers know they have a role to play in each step of the Customer-Buying process. They know where these steps take place, when they take place and whose involved. With these insights you're ready to develop an outstanding marketing strategy.

Analyzing your market

Analyzing a market means estimating how many potential customers you might be able to sell your products and services to. When analyzing any market, you want to group customers into four types. First are the customers that already buy from you. In fact, not only do they buy from you, they buy exclusively from you, and never from a competitor. The second group is similar to the first group in that they currently buy your products and services. The difference is these customers also buy products from your competitors.

Why? That's because for some categories of products, customers want choices. The clothing market is a good example. You almost certainly buy your clothes from many different manufacturers of clothes. The market for food is another example. The third group of customers are those that buy solely from your competitors, and never from you. At least not yet. And finally, the fourth group of customers are those that don't buy your type of product from anyone. We call them non-category users.

These potential customers are important, because acquiring them gives you a new source of revenue. Instead of taking market share from a competitor, getting these customers helps you increase the overall size of the market. Now, when we estimate the potential number of customers, that we might be able to capture for each of these four types. We do this so we can decide where we want to concentrate our marketing strategy. In marketing, it's the old adage, fish where the fish are.

It's a two step process. First, we estimate the total number of customers, then we make assumptions of what percentage we might convert to our brand. Let's do an example. Let's assume you are a maker of fine men's wallets. Let's also define a potential customer as men between the ages of 15 and 65 who will purchase a wallet within the next year. Let's assume men replace their wallet every five years. That means 20% of the overall market, will get a new wallet each year.

For group one, I use hypothetical numbers and say that, in the US market, our company has 25,000 loyal customers. You could get this sales data from retailers like Amazon, and your department stores. Next, let's look at group two, the so-called multi-brand customer. We call them that because the same products from multiple sources. In our wallet example, I don't know anyone that carries two wallets, so this market is virtually zero.

In group three are the customers who carry a wallet from competitors. In the US, there are about a hundred million men between the ages of 15 and 65. Let's keep this simple, and assume all of them carry a wallet. Finally, in group four, are the non-consumers of wallets. Given the assumption we just made before, i'll put zero here too. Now we need to estimate how many we might be able to get a sale from. Our company has 25,000 current customers, and one-fifth of them will be replacing their wallet this year.

So I multiply total customers times the conversion rate of 20%. That's 5,000 we already have who might be replacing their wallet this year. But in group 4, about 20 million of them will get a new wallet this year. So that's a pretty big market. Given this analysis, it's very clear that we would want to focus our marketing strategy on switching men from the competition over to our brand. If we can capture just 1% of that market, that's a potential for 200,000 new customers.

Once you're done with the market analysis, you've completed the analysis phase of the marketing planning process. It's time now to start crafting strategy.

3: Developing Your Strategy

Segmenting your customers

- If you've been following along with the earlier Chapters in this course, at this point of the marketing planning process, we've completed the analysis phase. We know a lot about our customers. We've estimated our market and where the most potential is. We understand our competition and we know how our products and services perform versus theirs. It's time to start the strategic phase of our planning. To create a marketing strategy, you have to perform three steps. First is segmentation, where you break your customers into homogeneous groups.

Next is targeting, where you decide which of these segments to go after. And finally is positioning, where you determine how you want your customers to think about your products versus the competition, so they're more likely to buy yours. Let's focus first on segmentation. Breaking customers into groups helps you be efficient with your marketing resources. It helps you focus only on the most relevant customers, and avoid wasting time and money on the less relevant.

There are four ways to segment a market. The first is demographic. This is where you group your customers by their characteristics such as income level, age, gender, or their height and weight. It's useful for certain products or services that deliver a benefit specifically tied to that characteristic. For example, if you're marketing a shampoo for redheads, then you would want to group customers by hair color.

Geographic segmentation groups customers by where they are physically. Knowing where your customers are helps you know where to place stores, for example, and where to communicate or sell to them. Behavioral segmentation is grouping customers by the things they do. It can be customer-related behavior such as how much they purchase, how frequently they purchase, or their price sensitivity. It can also be behavior such as hobbies or habits.

Finally, there is psychographic segmentation. This is grouping people by how they think, their attitudes and aspirations, especially about the benefits and ultimately the values that we explored in Feature Benefit Laddering. An example of psychographic benefit would be need for prestige or need for convenience. Segmenting this way tends to be very powerful. Let's take a look at our wallet example.

When we segment based on attitudes, we're looking for a benefit that meets three criteria: 1) our product actually delivers the benefit better than the competition; 2) customers perceive that our product delivers better; and 3) the benefit is rated highest in importance based on our customer analysis. If you find a benefit that meets these criteria, you select that as your segmentation variable.

You're going to base your whole strategy on this benefit and the features that deliver it. For our hypothetical wallet company, it looks like the benefit -- slim -- is the one to choose. But what do you do if you have this situation? Your product is superior at delivering the benefit, but customers don't rate it as very important. In that case, your strategy is still to emphasize that benefit but with the intent on raising the importance of it in the customer's mind.

You have to make a strong and compelling case why they should consider that benefit first when deciding whose product to buy. Another situation you could face is this: your product is superior at delivering the benefit but customers don't perceive it as better. Now your campaign will be to change the perception by giving them strong evidence of how your product compares head-to-head. In many situations, customers have to see it to believe it.

Targeting your customers

Segmentation tells us how we are going to appeal to customers. In targeting, we make decisions on whom to go after. It's a process of narrowing down your audience to a selected group. Now, that may seem like a bad idea. After all, the whole idea of marketing is to get as many customers as you can. Right? That's true, but keep in mind that your marketing message will not appeal to everyone.

You're better off narrowing down the audience to the most receptive ones, than blasting your marketing message to everyone, hoping that a few stick. You'll waste a lot of money that way. So, think of targeting as looking for the largest group of customers that are most willing to consider buying your product or service, based on your marketing appeal. When I do targeting, I start with the attitudinal benefit that we selected during segmentation. Then I test to see if there are any demographic characteristics of people that might be more inclined than others to want that benefit.

If there are, then I want to identify them, and market to them. I do the same thing with geographic data, or certain cities or countries, more likely to want that benefit. Next, I consider the behavioral data. Remember the four customer types we just described in the analysis phase? I look for two things. Which of the four groups is large in size, and might be most receptive to my marketing message? Let's do an example for our fictitious company, a maker of men's leather wallets.

Our primary benefit is slim. Now who out there might really, really value this benefit in a wallet? Older men? Younger? Heavy set? Thin and slim, well, probably not. I'm not coming up with any physical characteristics, who would want thin more than others. Let's move to behavioral. Our current loyal customers are already big believers in our thin message. Is there an opportunity to get more business out of them? Perhaps a passport case, or perhaps encourage them to buy it as a gift.

That's probably easy to do, but I have to balance that against the opportunity. The number of loyal customers is relatively small compared to the other customer groups. I could target customers who are using a competitor's wallet, and who may be ready to replace their wallet. There's a lot of them, and here's an idea. When I consider my primary benefit of thin, perhaps I need to expand my view of the customer definition. I'm not after men who are replacing their wallet.

Rather, I'm after men with over stuffed thick wallets. There's lots of them too. These guys are the most likely to appreciate the benefit of slimming down. Now here's my strategy. It's starting to take shape. I think of marketing as a set of dials on a control board, and I can turn those dials to get the right mixture of size, and probability of conversion. Think about how we define our core business, how we defined our scope. And customer definition.

And then, how we narrowed down our audience, using various segmentation approaches. Turning these dials to tweak our model gives us strategy, that defines how we are going to compete. And who we are going to compete for. We have one final step. We have to define what we are going to say to the market to convince them. That step is called positioning.

Positioning your message

Perhaps the most central idea in all of marketing is that of positioning. A company's value proposition is the single-minded claim that it makes to change the customer's mind, and cause them to do something. That something could be to buy a product, to try a product, or to pay a certain price. Maybe to visit a website. Or to think about your brand and its benefits in a certain way. How you position your product in the market will ultimately determine its success.

It may seem a little abstract, but positioning happens up here, in the mind of the consumer. Think of the consumer's mind as a three dimensional space. And in that space, they form opinions about products and services in a particular category. They have perceptions about which products perform better or worse on certain aspects. They consider certain features more or less important than others when deciding what to buy. And the good news is, as a marketer, you can change these beliefs.

You can move them in a new direction that increases the likelihood of buying your product. You do that by making a claim, and by supporting that claim with credible reasons to believe, or RTBs as we call them. Let's look at how. You'll find lots of different positioning tools and frameworks out there, but the one I prefer is this one. It's called the five box positioning tool. It was developed by an advertising agency called Leo Burnett, headquartered in Chicago, and it has lots of nice advantages over other frameworks.

Let's explore it. First, we define the current do, that is, what are the targeted customers doing today with respect to your product and the category you're in. Given that current do, what must their current belief about the products be, out there today? Next, given our strategy, what is it that you desire customers to do? What desired beliefs do you want them to have that will cause them to do the desired do? When I say beliefs, I mean the beliefs in opinions they have about your primary benefit, that you selected at the segmentation step.

Do they think it's important? How do they perceive your product versus the competition in delivering that benefit? Now the hard part. Given the current belief, and where you need to take them to believe the desire belief, what claim must you make? What supporting evidence do you have? Can you bridge that gap, or have you overreached a bit? Here's an example. Given our strategy, and our target audience, men with overstuffed, thick wallets.

Our current do is, I use a traditional wallet, and it's thick because of all the stuff I carry. The current belief is, I believe my wallet sticks out a lot, but all wallets are the same. Notice with each of the four boxes on each corner, that we write the statement using the first person. That of the customer. So we begin with I. The desired do is, I buy a slim wallet. The desired belief must be, I believe having a slim wallet carrying all the same stuff is rather clever.

The claim is, thin wallets are better designed than traditional wallets to carry all the stuff you have now, but be much slimmer. Is it believable? What evidence do we have to support that claim? Well, perhaps you could show side by side comparison of our wallets versus a traditional wallet carrying the same amount of stuff. Perhaps your website could have a video showing how the wallet is made, and include testimonials from actual customers on how much they like it.

The key will be to convince customers of the link between detailed features of the wallet to the benefits and values that we explored in our feature benefit ladder. Most importantly, they need to feel that a slim wallet is important, and that our wallet does it better than anyone else. That is good marketing.

Setting goals

- Marketing is about changing customers' beliefs so they prefer your products and services versus the competition. Ultimately, though, we're working towards a financial or other result to support your business. The final step of the strategy phase then is to set goals. Setting goals helps you in two important ways. First, goals help you decide how much marketing resource you'll need to devote to your tactical programs. The more aggressive goal you set, the more resources you'll need.

And second, goals help you measure your progress during the marketing campaign, to see if you need to make adjustments. Later in the course, I'll show you how to set up key performance indicators or KPIs and how they connect to the goals you set here. A marketing goal can be anything that's relevant to the success of the business. Most companies set a sales revenue goal, but it doesn't have to be dollars of revenue. You could set goals for number of units sold or perhaps market share or even number of new clients acquired.

If your cross-functional team includes a colleague from your finance department, consult with him or her on this. For a marketing goal to be the most useful, it should meet the following criteria. First, it should be specific. If you simply say your goal is to increase market share, that would not be specific enough. Increasing market share from 15% to 17% is much better, because it's specific.

Second, the goal should be measurable. Setting a goal that can't be measured will become frustrating for you and the team, especially when you try to gauge your progress in reaching it. Next, the goal must be attainable. Setting an unrealistically high goal won't do you any good. In fact, it could hurt your campaign by causing you to spend more marketing dollars than is warranted. The fourth criteria is relevant. That means the goal is directly related to your marketing strategy.

For example, let's look at our example from the wallet industry. Your targeting and five box positioning statement will tell you what types of customers you're trying to convert. Let's say that it's men with wallets from other manufacturers who will be buying a wallet within one year. Then the goal we set should specifically relate to capturing sales or units or market share related to those specific customers. That makes it most relevant.

And finally, the goal must be time-bound, meaning that the goal will be achieved during a specific period of time. That could be any time frame you want, but most likely, you'll set the same time frame for the same periods of time that your company measures financial results, a year, or perhaps a quarter, or even monthly. Taken together, these criteria spell the word, smart, and that's an easy and smart way to remember these important goal-setting criteria.

.

4: Developing the Tactical Phase

Understanding the 4ps model

Completing the STP process, segmentation, targeting, and positioning, gives you a clear idea of how you're going to compete, who you're going to target, and what you're going to say to the market to position your offering. Now, you have to bring that positioning to life, and you do that by creating and executing tactical marketing programs. In marketing, we use four types of tactical programs. Product and service, pricing, promotional communications, and distribution.

The last one, distribution, is sometimes referred to as place, because that's where we're deciding the places we need to put our product to get it to customers. Now, taken all together gives us product, price, promotion, and place. And you may recognize these as the famous four Ps of marketing. Let's review each one. By product and service programs, these refer to all of the aspects of how products and services perform their job in delivering benefits.

It includes things like the design of the product. How it feels to use it. The packaging of the product, and the people and processes involved in dealing with customers. It's not just how the product functions. But it includes the entire experience of buying and using it. That experience should be consistent with your positioning, and the brand promise. Pricing involves two things. Setting the actual price that customers will pay and communicating those prices in an effective way.

The price of your product or service implies their value that the consumer should expect from buying and using it. Promotion includes all the things you say outside of the company to the market. This is where you broadcast the value proposition and other information about the product. It includes, advertising, in-store promotions, email campaigns, social media, and sales promotions. And finally, distribution. These are the programs that create an effective pathway to get your product from the factory into the customer's hands.

Somebody has to take the product, ship it, store it, place it on the shelves, sell it, and possibly service it once the sale is made. All four Ps have to work together to convey the value proposition. No one of the four Ps can carry all the load. A good marketer uses all the tactical tools available to make the biggest impact possible.

Creating the right products and services

Marketing is all about delivering value to customers. And you do that by offering them the right products and services. Think of products and services as benefit delivery vehicles. They're a collection of various features that create value when customers use them. So, how do you build the right product or service? For that, you need to go back to the analysis phase of the marketing planning process. From there, you'll need the results of your product analysis.

That's where you did a detailed comparison of how your product compares to the competition's, feature by feature. You also created the feature benefit ladder, that unpacked the product to see how features connect to the benefits that customers seek. You will also need the customer analysis. Especially the market research on what factors are most important to customers when they buy a product, as well as the data on how they perceive your brand versus the competition. And finally, you'll need your marketing strategy, as expressed in your value proposition that we covered earlier.

As a marketer, you have to give your development team guidance on four aspects so they build the right product. First is, what features the product must have to compete against the competition and also satisfy the customer? You have to especially guide them on what features or feature to emphasize the most. Look at your value proposition. What benefit are you promising? Then look at your feature benefit ladder. Find that benefit on the ladder, then move down the ladder to find the set of features that deliver it.

You want to make sure those features are most evident when the customer uses the product. Next, your development team needs guidance on performance of each feature. Once again, your value proposition should guide you on whether the product needs to work better than, the same as, or slightly less effectively than the competition. Also look at your market research. If consumers perceive your product as less effective on a particular feature, you may need to have the development team increase its performance.

Your development team also needs guidance on design. Meaning the look and feel of the product or service. What does your brand stand for? Given that, what must your product or service look like to express that brand essence? Finally, your team must think of the product or service as an entire customer experience. Remember the customer buying process from earlier? Think of each step as a touch point where you, as the marketer, have an opportunity to figuratively touch the customer with something about your product or service.

Touch points include things like the service customers get in a store. And how your products are displayed. It also includes things like the packaging and perhaps the instructions on how to use the product. Everything the customer comes in contact with, including things online, are touch points. Based on their experience at each touch point, the customer will form beliefs about what your brand stands for, whether it's consistent, believable, and authentic.

The more authentic, the more loyal your customers will become. And that's a very good way to build your business.

Setting prices

- Setting prices is the quickest of the four P's, but that doesn't mean it's the easiest. In fact, making a mistake here can be very costly, in terms of lost revenue, as well as sending the wrong signal to the market about your products and services. Let's start with some definitions. To be successful at pricing, you need to understand the difference between a product's cost, its price, and its value. The cost of the product is all the direct and indirect expenses that you experience as the manufacturer to make the product.

Things like raw materials and labor, for example. Price is what a consumer has to pay to acquire the product. A price is a signal, a piece of information. About what, you might ask. About the value. Value is what the consumer gets out of the product, the collective set of benefits delivered by the product. The most common mistake in pricing is setting it based on your costs. It may seem counter-intuitive, but price is unrelated to costs.

Your customer doesn't care what it cost you to produce the product. They don't compare your costs to what they pay. Instead, they compare what they pay versus the total value they get from the product. If value exceeds price, then they'll buy the product, and if not, they'll ignore the product. Value-based pricing, then, is the process of calculating the total delivered value from using the product, then setting the price at or just below that amount.

Think of price as a shortcut. The price quickly tells a customer a lot about the quality and value. But what about the competition and their prices? Go back to the five box positioning tool and look at your value proposition. If your positioning your product as superior to the competition, then you should set the price higher than theirs. If your product is equivalent to the competition, make the price the same, and if your product is inferior to the competition, set the price lower.

That's how price becomes a signal of value in comparison to competitors' prices. Let's do an example. Let's imagine you're selling laptop computers. You have two competitors with comparable models, and one is priced at $1099, and the other is priced at $1599. If you compare the features of your model to theirs, you'll see that they differ in available memory, size of the hard drive, and processing speed.

It looks like your price will be somewhere in the middle, but where exactly? Well, it depends on how customers will value the difference in prices to the difference in features. You have an advantage over competitor A in memory space and hard drive space, so you want to price above them. You could buy that additional memory and storage space from third parties for around say $200. If you price more than that, customers could buy the model and possibly upgrade it on their own.

So, that puts your price at about $1299. What about competitor B's model at $1599? That would put it at $300 more than your price, if you keep it at $1299. For that additional amount, the customer gets twice the hard drive space and a little faster processing speed. If the customer thinks it's well worth it, you may need to lower the price a bit to make your model look like a better value. Here's a tip. Have you ever noticed how a lot of prices end in the number nine? Research shows that customers are more attracted to prices that end in the number nine.

So, it's a widely used pricing approach. Price is a signal of value and a powerful part of the four P's, so make sure you put it to effective use in your marketing campaign.

Communicating price

After you set the price of your product or service, you have to communicate it in an effective way that supports your overall strategy. A simple framework for this is answering the questions, who, what, why, when, and where. Your target audience, of course, is who you want to communicate to. But it's more than just potential customers. You also want to make sure your partners, such as distributors, understand your pricing structure. Generally speaking, you want to make your prices available to the public.

Including competitors. They may be setting their prices based on yours. What you communicate about pricing is much more than just the dollar amount. When a customer first sees the price, that's a critical time to remind them of the value they're getting for their money. Be sure to tell them about any discounts that might apply. Or any other terms and conditions, such as shipping and handling charges. You want customers to have a complete and clear picture of your pricing.

If they're confused about something, they may look elsewhere. And this is the main reason why you communicate price. Customers ask themselves a simple question. Am I getting my money's worth? You need to help them answer this question or they'll do it by themselves. And they may come up to the wrong conclusion. Customers try to calculate what they're getting by comparing the total value to the total price paid. The easier you make it for them, the more they'll understand your offering. When you communicate the price depends on several factors.

Remember the customer analysis in the steps of the buying process we talked about earlier? That analysis helps you understand what factors are most important when buying your product. If price is the most important factor, then you must communicate price very early in the buying process. If it's not the most important factor, then you want to communicate it later during the phase where customers are evaluating their alternatives. They key is to make sure they understand the value they get in all the features of the product or service before they get the price.

Where you communicate price depends on the point of sale, and where people go for information about your products. If customers do their research online, you'll need to have prices on a website, either yours or a distributor's. If your prices change very often, or you offer regular discounts, it may be best to disclose price at the same location the customer buys the product. Think about the touch points of the customer experience and where those occur physically.

Then, select a location for disclosing the price that helps the customer make the connection between price and value. Oh, and one final tip. Pricing is a business activity that is governed by certain laws. It's usually a good idea to have your legal advisors review the overall pricing approach to make sure you're in compliance.

Setting promotional objectives

In the four Ps model, promotion is where you communicate to the customer to get them to understand something, and ultimately to get them to do something. To create effective promotional programs, follow these steps. First, determine the objectives of the program. Second, select the message you want to communicate. Next, select the target audience to receive the message. Then, you select the media that will carry the message.

And finally, create the material that you send to the market. In this chapter, I'll describe step one. How to determine the objectives of your promotional effort. There are five communication objectives that you can try to achieve. Think of them as levels of awareness. First is called basic awareness. Customers need to know that your product or service exists, before they can even consider buying it. Basic awareness is achieved when the customer simply recognizes your product or service when they see it or hear it mentioned.

Basic awareness is essential for new products or for new features on existing products. Next is top of mind awareness. Now, the customer not only knows your product, but also would recall it first if they were asked to list the names of products in a particular category. To achieve this, you have to constantly remind customers about your product and that gets expensive. But it could be worth it. Having top of mind awareness can increase your sales significantly.

Once the customer has basic awareness of your product, now you want them to have information awareness. This is where the customer can actually explain something about your product to others. Perhaps about its features, its performance, or how to use the product. The fourth objective that you might want to achieve is called image awareness. That's achieved when the customer can explain your product, and also associate your product with some mental image. That image should be closely tied to the brand image you're trying to convey.

Ideally, the customer associates some image about themselves when they use or experience your product. Finally, your marketing communication objective might be to cause some type of behavioral awareness, where you're suggesting that they actually do something. That behavior may be as simple as going to your website. Or it might be more aggressive, such as asking the customer to buy the product. Notice how these objectives are more complicated and difficult to achieve as we go from basic awareness all the way to behavioral awareness.

It's typically more expensive as you set more difficult objectives. So, how do you determine your objective? Well, it depends on two things. What does your customer believe and understand about your product now? And, what is your strategy? Look back at your customer analysis. Based on your marketing research, you should have some idea about what benefits in a product are most important to customers. And you should know how they perceive your product's performance in delivering those benefits. Are there any beliefs about your products that you need to change? Now, look at your five box positioning tool.

Here, you'll find the information you need to set objectives, especially in the desired belief and desired do and, of course, in the value proposition itself. What are you hoping to communicate and how does that translate into one of our five promotional objectives? Here is an example for our wallet company. Given the value proposition, our promotional objective is information awareness. We want to communicate to customers enough so that they can explain how our wallets let you slim down.

Sending your promotional message

Once you've set the objective for your marketing communications, now you need to implement it. First, select the message you want to communicate. Then select the target audience to receive the message. Next select the media that will carry the message. And finally, create the material that you send to the market. The message you send to the market will include the value proposition as well as the evidence of why that claim is true. We call these the reasons to believe or RTBs.

Here's what I do to craft the message. I imagine I'm standing in front of a group of customers, and I'm going to explain my value proposition. I know what they already know about my product, so I role play and actually speak the words that I would use with these customers. Once I'm satisfied with my message, I write it down and edit it, sometimes with the help of a professional copywriter. Next, you need to select the target audience. This should be easy because you've already done this when performing the targeting step in STP.

Are you communicating to your current loyal customers, customers that are new to the category and so on. It's important to clarify this. When you send the message you need to do it in a way that the target audience knows it's for them. The media channel you select depends on the target audience, how many of them you want to reach, the complexity of the message you're sending, and how frequently they need to hear the message. Marketers have a wide choice of traditional media including, television, radio, print advertising, outdoor billboards, and digital media, which includes social media, websites and mobile channels.

Each type of media has advantages and disadvantages. TV commercials for example can reach millions of people, but it's expensive. Billboards on the other hand are not that expensive but they're limited in what objectives you can achieve. It would hard to explain how to use a complicated product in a billboard. You have to weigh the cost versus the reach, meaning, how many customers get the message. And you have to consider how much information you can send.

My advice is to match the medium to the message. Then, decide on how many people you have to reach based on your available budget. Now you're ready to actually create the marketing material to put into the market. That might be a new website, a print ad, or a commercial. Most companies use the services of a creative advertising agency for this, but you'll need to give them guidance on what you want. And you do that with a creative brief, which I'll cover later in this course.

Using social media to promote your products

Social media is an essential part of any marketing plan, no matter what business you're in. Consumers expect a way to learn about your products and share their experiences with others online. Social media is a powerful way to communicate your value proposition and enhance your brand.

So what I want to do here is give you guidelines on how to make sure you tie your social media programs to your marketing strategy. Otherwise, you might find yourself in a situation where social conversations are happening that are inconsistent with your value proposition. Or, worse, that are sending wrong information about your products and services. Effective marketers use social media in three ways. The first is to listen to the conversations that are taking place.

The second is to join the conversation. And the third is to shape the conversation. I call it the listen, join, and shape model. Let me explain each of these. Giant social media sites like Facebook, Twitter, and LinkedIn, as well as the smaller lesser known sites, are great sources of market information. But you have to set up systematic ways to monitor these sites to find out what customers are saying to each other. You have to put your ear to the ground so to speak.

Let's look at Twitter. Using the Twitter search function, type in the name of your product. See what tweets are coming across that mention your product. Do this for your brand and company name. You can also set up automatic monitoring of Twitter for these key words, using tools like Hootsuite. You can do the same for Facebook. And you should set up Google Alerts, using key words about your company, and perhaps your competitors. Set up RSS feeds, so that any mention of your product or brand on a website is fed to you automatically in an RSS reader.

Once you have the pulse of the social web by listening in, look for ways to join the conversation. That means get out there and participate in the dialog, but you have to do it in an authentic way. Don't disguise your identity. People will respect your comments and your company if you represent yourself and your company honestly. You should join the conversation when you have something relevant to say in response to a customer, or a potential customer on a social media site.

You may need to resolve a consumer complaint, or perhaps correct some misinformation. Do this in a friendly, helpful way, and you'll build a positive reputation for your company. Here's a tip. When dealing with a customer issue online, always keep in mind what other customers are going to think about the way you're handling it. If you're dealing with a sensitive issue, it may be best to ask the customer to contact you offline through traditional customer service support. Finally, you also have an opportunity to shape the conversation.

Share information that supports your value proposition. Go back to your promotional objectives and create comments on sites that support that objective. Be careful not to overpromote, or you'll just annoy people, and that defeats the purpose. In all cases, be sure to follow your company's social media policy on what you can and cannot do on the social web. Listen, join, and shape. Three effective ways to use social media, and increase the likelihood of success of your marketing strategy.

Understanding distribution Channels

Building distribution channels may be the most difficult of the four Ps, depending on your business. It's typically the most people-intensive aspect of your marketing effort, because you have to enlist lots of partners to move your products physically into the marketplace. A channel is a pathway that carries things, and it may involve many steps along the way. Three things move through it. First is your product. Typically your product flows from you, the manufacturer or reseller, through to the hands of the customer.

Occasionally, that product might move back the other way, in case the customer wants to return it. And you have to be set up for that. The other thing that moves through the channel is money. And it's not just money and credit cards, but also money-related parts of the transaction, which may include financing, negotiations, and perhaps contracting. You are your channel partners need to be skilled and available to do these things, again depending on your business.

There's one more thing that flows through the pathway. And in some respects, it may be the most important thing. That is, information. And it flows in both directions, from you to the customer, and vice versa. The information you send through the channel could be information about your product, your prices. Availability, or promotional messages about a new product. The channel, and all the partners in it play a vital role in communicating your value proposition.

In the other direction flows information about your customer. It might include demographic information, about who they are. Geographic information, about where they live. Perhaps feedback about your product, positive or negative. Earlier in the course, I spoke about segmentation. You could learn a lot of information about what's important to customers, and how they perceive your product versus the competition. Through this channel, you can learn vital information that would help you analyze your market to create your marketing strategy.

That's assuming that your partners along the way in the channel let you. Sometimes, they like to keep that information for themselves. They might see that customer as belonging to them, not you. If you want access to that wealth of data about your customers, you'll have to select your partners carefully, and strike the deal with them around collecting and sharing that information. And that's where managing channels get difficult. Conflict often arises in the channel, because the various partners have competing goals.

Your distributors, for example, may not like your pricing approach. So they might set the prices where they want them, and that price level might not be consistent with your value proposition. They may also be selling competitors' products. And you have to do a lot of convincing and nurturing to make sure your products get the right amount of attention. It takes a lot of work and energy to train and motivate your channel partners to do what's needed to put your strategy into motion. But if you do it right, you'll have a well oiled machine to put more great products into the marketplace, and earn new customers.

Designing distribution channels

A distribution channel has three objectives. It needs to deliver a product customers want, at a convenient location, and at convenient times, so that your marketing effort is successful. The right product means that you have the necessary inventory of product on hand, when the customer is shopping. That means you have to have all the models, and all the styles and sizes and available options that a customer might want at that moment. Missing just one of these will cause the customer to look elsewhere.

And you lose the sale. The people selling your product need to be skilled at merchandising it, and explaining it to customers. They might have to demonstrate the product, and explain why it's superior to others. The right location means that your product is conveniently located, and it's easy to find. The salespeople have to be skilled at transacting the purchase. If you have an online store, it too has to be easy to find, easy to locate a product, and easy to buy from.

Otherwise customers may look for a place that's more convenient. Your channel must offer quick delivery or fast service. It means you have convenient hours of operation, and customers don't have to wait to get access to your product. If you keep people standing in line too long, it erodes the experience they have with your brand, and they may abandon you. To design a channel, you have to decide three things. The length, the breadth and the depth. Length of channel means the number of intermediaries between you and the customer.

You may want to sell direct. Meaning the channel length is very short, it's just you and the customer, and it gives you total control of the channel. Or you may need to go indirect and hire partners to ship, warehouse, and sell your product. Breadth of channel means the number of outlets of each type of partner. Exclusive distribution means you have just a few outlets selling your product. A high end jewelry company, like Tiffany's, has just a few outlets.

Whereas a company like Starbucks has thousands. Depth of channel means how much of the channel you own and control, versus having a third party do it for you. Channels are expensive, and you might not have the resources or skills to do all of it, so you'll usually have to hire others to help. Imagine you work for a company that makes fine men's wallets. Let's design your channel. You sell wallets in many countries around the world. You're a small company, so you'll have to use an indirect channel, and hire various partners to get products into the marketplace.

How about breadth? Well, given your value proposition, you probably want to hand-pick some exclusive retail distributors in various countries. That can explain the benefits of your slim wallets, and sell them alongside other clever high quality products. The key is to integrate all four Ps to create a great tactical marketing program, and we'll explore that next.

Integrating all four Ps

The four Ps of marketing is an old and classic idea, but still very relevant. The mistake you can make is to not have all of them work together. You need to create marketing programs that are in sync with each other and support the overall positioning described in your strategy. It may seem obvious, but it can be more challenging than you think. Look at this example and see if you can spot what's wrong. Imagine your strategic positioning is to be the elite watch maker for the medium priced luxury watch market.

Your goal is to appeal to consumers who want to make a statement that they've achieved. Your product is a gold watch with Swiss movements and fine, sophisticated design. Your price point is $4,000. You promote the watch in premium magazines like Smithsonian, and then you sell the watch in thousands of discount department and drug stores. Do you see what's wrong here? Of course, it's the channel design that is completely inconsistent with the positioning.

Selling such an expensive watch right next to a $30 watch sends the wrong signal. People shopping for a $4,000 fine watch would expect to find it in exclusive jewelry stores. Not in a discount store. But channel design is not the only one of the four Ps that can go astray. Look at your product. A common mistake is to over feature the product or service. By adding many bells and whistles, you may be succumbing to a problem called feature creep.

You keep adding features to add more value, but that value is inconsistent with the value proposition. This can be a challenge for R&D or engineering teams who are motivated to make the product amazing. You, as the marketer, have to guide their development to keep it in line with strategy. Now, there may be times when your product development team comes up with an amazing breakthrough. A feature that changes the competitive balance. They find a way to make your product clearly superior to the competition.

Well, in that case, it may make sense to accept the change and go back and revise your value proposition to fit the product's profile. Pricing is another area that gives marketers problems. You want to resist this common mistake. Your product is better than the competition, and everyone knows it. It's tempting to say, hey, my product is better than theirs. If I price it lower than theirs, I'm going to win big. Wrong.

Pricing a superior product lower than the competition sends the wrong signal, and it confuses customers. They'll pay more for more value, so make sure to line the price up so it communicates more value. Finally, is your promotional part of the four Ps. You should promote your product or service only where customers expect to see it. It's tempting to put the word out about this great new product or service through mass media to get the widest exposure possible, but once again, if you promote your product where the customer doesn't expect to see it, they may get confused and walk away.

Your value proposition doesn't sink in. Think of the four Ps this way. Each is an oar of a rowboat. Make sure all are rowing at the same time and speed and you'll get to your final destination a lot faster.

5: Aligning the Organization

Presenting to leadership teams

An effective marketing plan is one that lays out a coordinated set of strategies and tactics to win in the marketplace. At some point in the process, you'll need to gain support for that plan. And perhaps the most important audience is your senior management. They're the ones, typically, who allocate financial and human resources to various projects in your company. Without their full support, you may end up not getting what you need. Here are some tips on how to make a big impact with senior leaders when presenting your marketing strategy.

First, try to lead with a story. Perhaps focus on a customer who had a great result using the product. This is a great way to remind people how your products bring value to customers. Next, share what's changed in the marketplace. What new threats, new products or trends are out there that are creating a challenge. We call this creating the burning platform. You want people to understand the difficult situation you're up against. Then share the process you went through to create the marketing plan.

Give credit to your team members. It builds your credibility when you've collaborated with a cross-functional team. Be as brief as possible, because you probably won't have a lot of time. You should be prepared with different length presentations. For example, you should have a 10 minute version, a 30 minute version and a one hour version. Savvy marketers also know how to present their strategy in 30 seconds or less, the so-called elevator speech. After all, it's all about getting people on board.

You don't have to share every detail about your plan, just the highlights. Present the market conditions, the competitive situation, your strategy in terms of who you're targeting and how your positioning approach will convert customers. Be completely up front about the weaknesses or risks with your plan. You gain trust when you're up front and honest about potential issues. Then, share your forecasted revenue and budget needs. Make sure they completely understand your assumptions.

Take your time here. If you see that someone has a different view around the assumptions, clarify it on the spot. Not aligning around the assumptions now can create real problems for you later. Remind them that funding your marketing plan is an investment, not a cost. Assure them that you're committed to getting them a good ROI. Given their experience, be sure to ask them for feedback on ways to improve your plan. Finish the presentation by asking them for their support.

It's the old sales adage, always ask for the order. You're there to get approval, so look them straight in the eye and ask for it. Great marketers show passion and enthusiasm for the products and services they manage. If your senior managers see that you're excited and confident, you're going to win them over.

Educating the sales team

If your company has its own sales force or a network of distributors, they'll need to understand your marketing strategy. After all, they play a key role implementing it. This is a great opportunity for you to help make sure your plan is successful. There are two things that you need to do with sales people. Motivate and educate. You need to win the hearts and minds of the sales force, and get them engaged in telling your story correctly.

If they feel good about your product and confident they can sell it, they'll do a great job for you. Your written marketing plan should have all the information you need to educate your sales team, but don't just make copies of the plan and pass it out, it's much more effective to create a concise and motivating training session. The first thing they need to know is your strategy, especially your value proposition. They should know who the target market is, and they should know where and how to find them.

Share your customer analysis with them, what buying factors are most important to the target audience? Once they understand your strategy, give them the tactical tools they need to sell the product. First, they need to understand how the product works, and how it compares, feature by feature, to the competitor's product. If possible, have samples of the products so they can work with them hands-on, side by side. Next, share your pricing strategy and how prices are communicated.

Explain how the price was determined in relation to the value delivered. You might get some resistance here because sales people generally like the prices to be low. That's why it's essential they understand how pricing supports the overall positioning. Finally, share any selling tools you've created to make their job easier. These can include product brochures, or tools to demonstrate the product. You might even have a suggested selling script for them to use. When you conduct training for sales people, here are some suggested tips.

First, you may want to break the team in to different experience or skill levels. That helps you deliver appropriate information to each group. Consider using hands-on training and role playing exercises. Perhaps let them practice how to demonstrate the product, and engage prospective customers. Speaking of customers, see if you can invite some customers to the training. If not, consider sharing testimonials of customers talking about how much they like the product. Another good technique is to use one of your most successful sales people to help with the training.

Let them share a case study of a sales person who has already sold the products successfully. Sales people will see your message as more credible if it comes from of their own colleagues. Repetition is the key for training a sales force. Consider regular webinars as a way to continue to engage the sales force and fine tune their training. Finally, make sure the sales team has a point of contact if they have questions or concerns. If the sales team feels they have your full support, they'll work hard to make the product a big success.

Guiding vendors and agencies

Your strategy may include the creation of marketing materials, like advertising, promotions, websites, and sales literature. If so, you'll probably use some type of external agency or an internal team to help you. To do a great job for you, they need your guidance and you do that with what's called a creative brief. A creative brief is a short overview of a creative assignment. A good creative brief sets expectations for the project.

It answers key questions like, what needs to be created? How will it be used? What are the deliverables for the project? And when are the deadlines? It's like a contract. You can find many templates online for creative briefs Whatever format you use, it should include the following. First, give an overview of your marketing situation. What's the big picture? What's going on in the market? What's the competition doing? Are there any opportunities or problems in the market? Next, describe the objective of the creative piece.

Is it a commercial? A sales brochure? A website? And so on. Give a concise statement of the effect that it should have on consumers. Then, describe the target audience. Who are we talking to? The more precise and detailed you can be, the better. Explain how the audience currently thinks, feels, and behaves in relation to the product category, your brand, and your specific product or service. Next, outline the most important thing to say. That, of course, is in your value proposition. It's the single most persuasive statement we can make to achieve the objective. You should also include the reasons to believe. What are the supporting rationale and emotional reasons to believe and buy? The agency may use these points in the creative piece. Then, describe how you'll measure success. What specific metrics will you look at to see if the creative piece is working? Is it website visits? Is it units of products sold? Or it could be something you measure later with marketing research like top-of-mind awareness.

Complete your creative brief with a schedule and a budget for the project. Notice that every bit of the information that goes into the creative brief can be found in your marketing plan. Segmentation, targeting, positioning, consumer analysis, communications objectives, and so on. It's all there. But keep in mind that the creative brief should be, well, brief. Don't just hand the agency your marketing plan and expect them to sort through it.

A creative brief is much more detailed than your plan, but very focused on just one specific marketing program in that plan. With the proper guidance from a well-written creative brief, your support teams will create amazing and effective marketing materials.

6. Launching and Measuring your Plan

Budgeting

Marketing takes time and money. So, it's important that you develop a budget. A good budget helps you allocate the right amount of resources to the right marketing programs. Now, there are two ways to develop a budget. You can decide on how much you have to spend, in total, and then allocate it. Some companies do this by taking a percentage of sales revenue as the total budget for marketing. That amount is assigned to different teams and programs. I call this the top down approach.

The other approach is from the bottom up. Each marketing team develops a budget to spend on marketing programs that they think are needed to achieve a revenue forecast. Those budgets are combined into a company-level budget. If you recruited a finance member to your marketing planning team, they'll be able to tell you what approach your company uses. Whichever approach you take, you still need to decide where to spend the money and how much to spend. One thing's for sure. You always have a limited amount of money to spend, so you probably can't do all the things you'd like to.

But be careful of a common mistake, don't take your limited dollars and spend a little amount on many different programs. If you spread your budget too thin, you won't give any tactical program a chance to succeed. It's better to limit rather than dilute. Spend on those programs that are likely to be most effective at positioning your product in the marketplace. How much you spend depends on a number of factors. Earlier, we looked at how many customers are in your target audience. The more you have to reach, the more you'll have to spend. We also addressed how to position the product in the market, meaning how to change the customers' sense of importance and perception about your brand. If your positioning is very aggressive and requires the consumer to change behaviors in a significant way, you're going to need to spend more money.

Finally, look at each of your tactical programs, the four Ps. Product, price, promotion and place. Estimate the required spending in each one. For example, do you need to spend money to upgrade your product or its packaging? How much do you need to spend on marketing communications to reach a sufficient number of people and still achieve the communications objective? What do your distributors and sales people need to do their job effectively? Once you have estimated what each program will cost, you'll probably need to make some tough choices, and this is a great time to use the talents of your marketing planning team.

Let them help you decide. In my experience, a team decision ends up being better than any single individual decision. After all, you're in this together. So, put them to work in helping you develop the most effective budget possible.

Measuring key performance indicators (KPIs)

Before you launch your marketing campaign you want to set up key performance indicators, or KPIs for short. Key performance indicators help you keep track of your overall strategy and your individual marketing programs. They alert you when it's time to intervene. And take action to get things back on track. Without KPIs, you're flying blind so to speak, and you run the risk of falling short of your overall goal. To be most effective, each KPI should be quantifiable and measurable.

You can have as many as you want. But don't measure a KPI just because you have the data. If you're not going to use, don't bother. It's a waste of time. Measure something only if you plan to take action from it. That's why we set thresholds around each one. Each KPI should have a target of what you expect to happen. Plus a high and low number around that target. For those thresholds, you and your planning team should agree in advance what action you'll take if those thresholds are exceeded.

Here's an example. Assume you create a KPI around the number of new customers acquired each month. You set your target at 500. And also specify a high and low threshold of 600 and 400, respectively. If your actual customers per month is more than 600, you might consider taking action such as reducing advertising spending. On the low end, if you're below 400, you could consider increasing sales incentives.

Now, each KPI should be linked to the key parts of your marketing plan, including your goal, segmentation, targeting, positioning, and marketing tactics. For the goal, you might have KPIs around the timing of revenues. The type of customers you're converting,. And whether you're taking customers from the right competitor. For segmentation, targeting and positioning, you want to measure changes and customer beliefs, such as importance and perception. You may also want to measure their behaviors. Such as, purchase habits, customer attrition and retention profile. You need to carefully monitor whether you're achieving the market positioning that you had hoped for. For marketing tactics, you could create a KPI for each of the four Ps, if needed. For example, you might have measures around communications objectives, sales force effectiveness. Distributor activity, store promotions, search engine ratios, social media activity. Pricing and discounting rates, product performance, waiting times, and service complaints. Good marketers not only reach their financial goals. But they also know whether those goals were achieved the way they expected them to be achieved. They also take immediate action when they detect something is going in the wrong direction. KPIs help you and your marketing team stay aligned, and do what's needed to succeed

- Social media is an essential part of any brand building effort, no matter what business you're in. Consumers expect a way to learn about your products and share their experiences with others online. Social media is a powerful way to communicate your value proposition and enhance your brand. The most valuable and respected brands in the world use digital channels for brand building. Cocoa-Cola, for example, uses Facebook, Twitter, Instagram, Tumblr, and other channels, and these are all integrated around its main social platform, a website called Coke Journey.

According to Coke, its mission is to inspire moments of optimism and happiness and build our brands. To use digital channels effectively, follow these guidelines. First, make sure all the sites have a common look and feel. They don't have to be identical in their design, but they must adhere to the standards defined in your brand book. That means all logos, trademarks, colors, font styles, and typography are exactly per standard, otherwise you may confuse customers if a social media site doesn't look like the brand.

Second, be sure all sites use the same voice of the brand. The tone and style of writing should be consistent with the brand's personality. Third, be sure to define who can and cannot post things to the various social media sites. It's essential they be properly trained on the brand and how to communicate the brand's values and how to comply with the company's social media policies. Finally, be sure to specify the role of each social media site.

Overall, they exist to support the core brand promise, but individually they might each have a different role, and for that you need to refer to your list of brand drivers. Each social media site is another touchpoint in the customer experience, and just as you do with your other touchpoints, you can link each social media touchpoint to a different brand driver. Let's do an example with our case study, the ParentWatch. Our overall brand promise is, The ParentWatch celebrates parenthood by helping moms and dads be the very best they can be.

But I'm going to create my brand's Facebook page to be all about this brand driver. How busy parents do the impossible by balancing tasks and getting it all done in a day. It'll be full of helpful tips on all the things parents do. The brand's Twitter feed will be about high profile moms and dads and their successes. The Pinterest board, on the other hand, will be full of inspirational quotes about parents and how important they are to their families. I'll also create a mobile campaign, where moms and dads can opt in to receive helpful tips on teaching their kids important life lessons.

Pretty cool. So take a look at your digital channels. Make sure they adhere to the brand book, that they have a specific role tied to a brand driver, and that they are properly managed. Taken together, social media sites create a community of brand-loyal customers who interact with each other and with your company. That's the foundation for a strong customer relationship.

Calculating break-even points

Imagine you create a new promotional program that's going to cost $50,000. Should you spend it? Will you generate enough new sales to at least cover this cost? Because if you don't, you're wasting money. As a marketer, you need to be able to make these types of decisions and you do that with a tool called the break-even analysis. It allows you to estimate how many units of a product you need to sell in order to break even, assuming a given price and cost structure for the product.

That amount is called the break even point. If you sell less than that, you lose money,. But every unit sold over that is making you a profit. Here's the formula for break-even analysis. Break-even point equals fixed cost divided by unit selling price minus variable costs. This part with in the parentheses is also called the contribution margin. It's how much net cash you pocket after paying the variable costs of a product.

Let's do an example. Imagine you're selling men's wallets. You want to promote one of your wallets that sells for $89. To manufacture and sell the product, you have to spend $29 per wallet on things like labor, materials and sales commissions. If you want to spend $50,000 on that promotional program, your break-even point is calculated as follows. Our spending amount is $50,000. We subtract $89 minus $29, giving us a $60 contribution margin.

We divide $50,000 by $60 to give us 834 units, which is our break-even point. So what, you might ask. Well, the first question you ask is, will this promotion program generate at least 834 units of new sales? That means incremental. Over and above what you're already selling. If not, don't do the program, unless you can figure out how to change the promotional program so that it's more effective.

Now, keep in mind that your sales objective is to sell a lot more than just the 834 units to break even. And this is where your cross-functional marketing planning team can help. Especially your finance partner. They'll help you with forecasting and estimating the contribution margin. Now, there's always risk in running a marketing program, but you'll make better and smarter decisions about your marketing budget with this handy little tool called break-even analysis.

Calculating Customer lifetime value

Imagine a hypothetical scenario where you're forced to make a choice between acquiring two customers, which one would you choose? Well, it depends on how much they buy from you, if she spends more money on your products than he does, you'd select her. But wait a minute. What if she costs you more in terms of selling and customer service? She may spend more, but you actually earn less on her than on him. So then you would switch because the net profit is higher.

But hold on again. There's one more factor you have to consider. You make less profit on her, but what if you expect to retain her for a longer period of time than you retain him? You make more profit on one sale from him, but if you can continue selling to this lady for the next ten years, then you'll do much better. The way you make this type of decision in reality is with a tool called Customer Lifetime Value, or CLV for short.

CLV is the formula that helps the marketing manager arrive at the dollar value associated with the long term relationship with any given customer. It tells you just how much a customer relationship is worth over a period of time. Now, there are various formulas to calculate CLV, and some are more complex than others. The simplest way to estimate lifetime value for a typical customer is the following equation, unit selling price minus your variable costs times the number of repeat purchases per year times the average retention time in years.

Let's do an example. Imagine you're selling men's wallets. Your wallet sells for $89 and it costs you $29 to make and sell it. The typical customer buys a new wallet every three years. And you expect to retain him for an average of 20 years. The CLV formula gives us $89 minus $29 times 0.333 times 20 years equals a CLV of $400. So what? Well, calculating the CLV helps in several ways. First, it tells us that we wouldn't want to spend any more than $400 acquiring and retaining any one customer. Spending more than that, and we start losing money. It also helps you decide which customers are more valuable to acquire and retain. Like our example earlier. CLV encourages marketers to focus on the long term value of customers instead of investing resources in customers of lower value. And it makes you sensitive to how much you're spending on acquiring and retaining customers and whether it's effective.

.

7.Conclusion

Addressing organizational challenges

Marketing operates in a world of ambiguity. Every marketing situation faces some uncertainty, and you need to be prepared when unexpected things happen. If you're not prepared, your strategy may derail, and you end up losing competitive ground in the marketplace. Sometimes those unexpected events happen internally. The priorities in any organization are constantly shifting. You many have had everyone's support for your programs, only to find out that something's changed.

And now, some other parts of the business are getting more attention. You may also have to face some disruptive factors, like a company reorganization, or cutbacks in budgets and head count. You may face some challenges with other departments. For example, what are you going to do if your new product is behind schedule, causing you to miss the launch date? What if there are delays in manufacturing or shipping your products, and you can't get enough product on the shelves? That's a huge problem. What if there's a quality problem with a product or service, and your customers start complaining? You must react to that.

Problems can occur externally as well. Things are always changing in the marketplace. New competitors emerge. New regulations or legal actions might affect your ability to market a product. A bad customer experience may be going viral on social media sites. You wake up one morning, and find that your company is on the front page of the business section, and it's not good news. So here are some tips to help you cope with these types of challenges. First, be nimble.

You have to act fast when these things pop up. You don't want to let a small problem, become a big problem. Your managers will appreciate when they say that you're on top of it. So, act fast. Next, gather information. What's changed to cause this problem? Make sure you separate fact from fiction. You don't want to react to bad information, or just assume you know what's going on. What may have been the truth before, may not be anymore. Seek advice, especially from credible experts.

You need to leverage the brainpower of others. That'll help you prevent from getting tunnel vision, around the problem or possible solutions. Next, get into the solution mode. By that I mean, stop wishing the problem will go away. Develop a list of possible alternatives. Then work with your team on selecting and implementing the best one. Work on the things you can change, and avoid the ones you can't. Now be flexible here. You may have to give up on certain aspects of your plan to keep things moving forward.

If you dig in too hard, you can make your situation worse. Finally, look for ways to innovate. My experience suggests that the best way to revitalize a struggling marketing campaign, is to unlock new value. If the organization is stuck, use systematic creativity methods to generate new opportunities for your business. And that's what great marketers do. They help lead the company forward, especially in challenging times.

Mastering marketing thinking

Whether you spend your entire career in marketing, or just part of it, you'll find marketing to be a fascinating and challenging area of the business to work in. Like any profession, you need to continue to develop your skills. Given the changes in technology, and emerging trends. You have to constantly update your skills or they'll get stale. When I give career advice, I remind people to never let a year go by without developing some part of your professional skill set.

Now here are some tips on how to continue mastering your marketing skills. First, you need to decide where you want to focus. I think of marketing as a continuum over three phases. You can work in the early opportunity phase, which includes things like new Product development, Innovation, Design, and Marketing research. In the strategy phase you're involved in activities like Marketing strategy, Brand development, and Market expansion.

If you work in the execution phase, you're involved in things like Sales, Advertising, Pricing, and Retailing. You can have a gratifying career anywhere along this continuum, but once you find out what you like the best focus on it and put all your development efforts towards that. If you spread your training over too many areas, you may dilute your skills. Next, dive deep into that area and study the classic, as well as the new academic research about it.

Always think of yourself as a student of marketing. Read about what other companies are doing. Stay on top of new technology, watch for new trends, especially using social media tools. Remember that marketing is all around you, so take advantage of it. When you see a new product in a store or you see a commercial on TV, try to figure out the marketing aspect of it and what the strategy of the company is trying to use. That really builds your marketing muscle. If you consider yourself a marketer, then I advise you to join the community of practice.

Get out there and engage in organizations like the American Marketing Association, or the Product Development and Management Association. There's a professional society for just about every aspect of marketing, whether it's retailing, sales, pricing. There's even one called SCIP, the Society of Competitive Intelligence Professionals. These organizations are a great way to network and learn new skills. And finally, be sure to practice your craft.

Learning is a process of taking an action, reflecting on what happened, learning from it, and then improving for the next time. You want to learn at a rate faster than the rate of change. That means you need to experiment, practice new techniques while perfecting the old ones. If you do this on a continuous basis, you'll find a career in marketing even that much more rewarding.

Next steps

Sometimes marketing gets a bad reputation, especially when those darn telemarketers call your house right at dinner time. But let me assure you that not all marketers are bad, in fact, marketers and the marketing function serve a very important role in business and our society. Let's think about what marketers do. They create of lead the development of great new products and services. They work hard to discover unmet consumer needs. They create elaborate distribution channels to get products to you.

They convey valuable information about products and services, making it easier for you to shop and buy. Life would be very different without marketing. Look around you, you wouldn't have most of the products or services available to you today without the marketing function. The bottom line is that marketers create value so people can lead a better quality of life. But what really defines a great marketer is the one who practices it ethically.

So, in this final chapter, I want to share with you a set of guidelines to practice marketing in a professional way. So that you always do the right thing. If you follow these rules, you'll learn the respect of everyone in the market and you'll be more successful in the long run. Rule number one is, put the customers' interests first. Marketing is sometimes defined as creating and keeping a customer. And you do that by thoroughly understanding your customers and finding better ways to serve their needs.

Rule number two, put the best-quality products and services into the market that are safe and effective. That means that you offer products that you're proud of, that you have thoroughly tested. And that you're willing to stand behind. Rule three, avoid stereotyping customers. Market segmentation can lead you to the trap of making sweeping conclusions about people of different backgrounds. Demographic segmentation, especially, can get us into trouble.

Instead, base your segmentation on the needs that customers seek when using a product or service. Rule four, always charge fair prices. Base your prices on the value that your products deliver. Don't try to conceal hidden fees or other means of deceiving customers on what they have to pay for the product. Related to that is rule five. Be sure you communicate information that is accurate and complete. Be honest and truthful about what the product can and cannot do.

Don't exaggerate or make false claims. Let consumers try out your products first and help them in every way possible to get the most use out of it. Rule six, avoid undue influence. Never try to manipulate the customer. This is especially true for consumers that are more susceptible, like children, and the elderly. Rule seven, be a fair competitor. Never take unfair advantage of another company or do things that disparage or belittle them.

Competition's tough. But that doesn't mean you can't take the high road, fight the fair fight. Rule eight is, do no harm. When you put products and services into the market, think about the impact on communities, on families, and the environment. Think about the effect on people's health. How will these products be disposed of one day and what are the consequences? And finally, be accountable. Things go wrong at times, so you must have the courage and ethical sense to stand up and take responsibility when mistakes happen.

If you do, you'll be seen as a trustworthy and capable marketer who's making the world a better place.

Printed in Great Britain
by Amazon